Original title:
Sacred Ties

Copyright © 2024 Swan Charm
All rights reserved.

Author: Mirell Mesipuu
ISBN HARDBACK: 978-9916-89-220-6
ISBN PAPERBACK: 978-9916-89-221-3
ISBN EBOOK: 978-9916-89-222-0

Tapestries of The Unknown

In shadows deep where whispers tread,
The stories weave, though words are fled.
Threads of silence, colors blend,
A tapestry where dreams suspend.

Each stitch a secret, softly spun,
In the fabric of what can't be done.
Mysteries linger, frail yet bold,
In patterns hidden, tales unfold.

Underneath the moonlit sky,
The unknown dances, none deny.
Echoes gather, soft and fleet,
In the heart where fears retreat.

We gather stories, near and far,
In our minds, they shine like stars.
Woven paths, where futures glow,
In the depths of the unknown flow.

Through the silence, visions call,
Inviting us to cross the hall.
To glimpse the threads that hold our fate,
In the tapestry, we navigate.

Whispers Across Time

In shadows where the echoes play,
Old stories linger, night and day.
Voices soft as morning dew,
Reveal the past, both old and new.

Through coffers filled with tales unsaid,
Laughter dances, like threads of red.
We wander paths where memories chime,
Together still, we cross through time.

The Alchemy of Affection

In the crucible of tender hearts,
Love transforms, and never departs.
A spark ignites, a flame will soar,
Gold from silver, forever more.

With every glance, a potion brewed,
Life's finest flavors, sweetly stewed.
Two souls entwined in rhythmic dance,
Creating joy from happenstance.

Haven of Shared Dreams

In twilight's calm, our visions blend,
As we journey, hand in hand, my friend.
A sanctuary where hopes take flight,
Bathed in the glow of starlit night.

Each whispered wish ignites the skies,
Painting the heavens, where solace lies.
Together we shape what none can see,
In this haven, just you and me.

Heartstrings Like Vine

Through tangled paths, our spirits curl,
With every touch, emotions swirl.
In the garden of our heart's design,
Love grows wild, heartstrings like vine.

Each moment shared, a petal falls,
In fragrant whispers, the nature calls.
Bound together, we weather the storm,
In unity's embrace, we find our form.

A Tapestry of Connection

Threads woven tight,
In the colors of time.
Each stitch a story,
Binding hearts in rhyme.

Whispers of laughter,
Echo through the years.
Shared moments glimmer,
Bringing joy, not tears.

Underneath the stars,
We find our way home.
In the fabric of life,
We are never alone.

Stitch by stitch we grow,
In patterns of love.
A tapestry rich,
Crafted from above.

Together we stand,
In the warmth of the light.
Each connection a spark,
Illuminating the night.

Heartbeats in Harmony

Two souls intertwined,
In a dance of the heart.
Beats sync with the moon,
A rhythm, a start.

In silence we speak,
In glances we share.
Harmony flows,
In love's gentle air.

With every heartbeat,
The world fades away.
In the pulse of our bond,
We find joy's deep sway.

A melody forms,
With whispers of grace.
Together we bloom,
In this sacred space.

Every moment we hold,
Is a note in the tune.
Heartbeats in harmony,
Beneath sun and moon.

Unfurling Possibilities

In the garden of dreams,
Seeds of hope take flight.
Petals of promise,
Unfurl in the light.

Every dawn brings fresh hope,
A canvas so wide.
Brushstrokes of courage,
With passion as guide.

We dive into change,
With hearts open wide.
Unfurling new paths,
With each step, we glide.

In the dance of the now,
We find what awaits.
Possibilities bloom,
As we open the gates.

Together we blossom,
In the warmth of the sun.
Unfurling our futures,
As our journey's begun.

Journeys Together

With hands clasped tight,
We set forth as one.
Through valleys and peaks,
Our adventure's begun.

Each step on this path,
Leads to moments so grand.
A tapestry woven,
In the shifting sand.

The road may be long,
But our spirits stay high.
With laughter as fuel,
We reach for the sky.

In the trials we face,
Together we rise.
Through storms and through calm,
We find our reprise.

Journeys together,
Create memories bright.
In the heart of our bond,
We find pure delight.

Ties Beyond Time

Through ages past, our stories weave,
In whispers soft, we still believe.
Though miles apart, hearts intertwined,
In shadows cast, our love aligned.

Memories dance upon the breeze,
A timeless bond that never flees.
In laughter shared and tears we shed,
The ties we hold, forever spread.

In twilight's glow, our spirits rise,
While starlit nights unveil the skies.
We journey on, though paths may part,
For you, my love, reside in heart.

Across the years, through stormy skies,
Our anchor holds, as hope supplies.
In dreams we meet, no end in sight,
Our souls entwined in love's pure light.

The Unseen Thread

A gentle touch, an echo faint,
In silence speaks the heart's complaint.
With every glance, a world is spun,
Two lives entwined, forever one.

Invisible threads of fate are drawn,
In twilight's kiss, we greet the dawn.
No matter where the journey leads,
This bond we share, a heart that breeds.

Though storms may rage and shadows creep,
In faith we stand, our promises keep.
Through laughter's joy and sorrow's test,
In unseen threads, we find our rest.

Whispers linger on the breeze,
A tapestry crafted with ease.
In every heartbeat, dreams conjoin,
A sacred space where love's aligned.

Kin of the Heart

In bonds of love, we find our kin,
A family forged from deep within.
Through trials faced, our spirits grow,
In unity, our strength we show.

Through seasons change, we stand as one,
In laughter shared, and battles won.
Hand in hand, we face the tide,
In every tear, our hearts confide.

The ties we share run deep and true,
In every moment, I cherish you.
A bond that time cannot erase,
In kinship's heart, we find our place.

In love's embrace, we journey far,
Through light and dark, you are my star.
Together we'll write our own tale,
In kin of the heart, we shall prevail.

Celestial Embrace

Beneath the stars, we find our way,
In cosmic dance, our hearts will sway.
A universe of dreams ignites,
In celestial glow, our souls take flight.

With every heartbeat, galaxies spin,
Inside your gaze, I'm drawn within.
In stardust trails, love's light cascades,
Through time and space, our bond pervades.

From dusk till dawn, we shine anew,
In every glance, my heart finds you.
In cosmic realms, we intertwine,
A love so vast, a fate divine.

As comets streak across the night,
Our dreams align in sheer delight.
In this embrace of endless skies,
Together, love, we shall arise.

Ties of the Ancients

In the shadow of the mountains,
Whispers of the past unfold,
Roots entwined in ancient soil,
Stories of the brave and bold.

Through the echoes of the ages,
Wisdom flows like rivers bend,
Carrying the strength of lineage,
Binding every heart and friend.

In the warmth of sacred fires,
Legacies dance in the night,
Guiding souls through darkened lands,
In unity, we find our light.

Every tale a thread unspooled,
Woven deep in time's embrace,
Honor sung in every heartbeat,
In our veins, the past finds place.

Thus we gather, hand in hand,
A circle formed, a vow ignites,
Through the ties of ancient whispers,
We stand strong in shared delights.

Resilient Connections

Roots run deep beneath the surface,
In the earth, a hidden strength,
Branches sway with gentle breezes,
Reaching out at every length.

Through trials faced, we rise together,
Facing storms with hearts aligned,
Every bond a shining beacon,
In the dark, our hopes entwined.

Walls may rise and rivers widen,
But our spirits know no bounds,
In the heart of every struggle,
Resilient love is always found.

Through laughter shared and tears embraced,
Connections forged in seamless light,
We find solace in each other,
Chasing shadows, seeking bright.

As seasons change and paths diverge,
We remember where we've grown,
In each other, strength unyielding,
Resilient hearts will find their home.

Echoes of Affinity

In the silence, whispers linger,
Softly calling from the past,
Voices blend like gentle music,
Creating bonds that hold us fast.

Every glance a spark ignites,
In the warmth of shared delight,
Harmony in laughter echoes,
Guiding hearts through day and night.

Though the world may shift and tremble,
We remain a steady flow,
Echoes of our affinity,
Carried where the wild winds blow.

In every hug and fleeting moment,
A tapestry of love is spun,
Threads of joy and understanding,
Binding all, we are just one.

So let us cherish every heartbeat,
Each connection, pure and true,
In the echoes of affinity,
Our souls dance, always anew.

Tapestry of Togetherness

Threads of gold and shades of blue,
Woven close, a vibrant seam,
In the fabric of our stories,
We discover faith and dream.

Every hand a skilled creator,
Stitching moments, hearts aligned,
In this tapestry of life, dear,
Every face a treasure bind.

Through the trials, threads pull tighter,
Life's design a work of art,
In the warmth of shared creations,
Lies the beating of one heart.

Colors bright, they dance together,
Patterns formed with love and grace,
In this woven world, forever,
Every stitch a sacred place.

So let us craft a brighter future,
In the light, our spirits rise,
Together, we'll weave the wonder,
In the tapestry of skies.

Bridges of Belonging

Across the waters, shadows play,
A dance of souls, come what may.
We forge these ties, unseen but strong,
In every heart, we find our song.

Hand in hand, we build our way,
Paths entwined, night and day.
Whispers of hope, echoes of grace,
Together we find our rightful place.

Beneath the arching sky so wide,
We cast our fears, we turn the tide.
The laughter shared, the tears that blend,
With every step, we near the end.

Through storms that rage, through clouds that part,
We weave our dreams, a work of art.
Bridges made from love's embrace,
In this journey, we find our space.

So take my hand, let's wander free,
In this world, just you and me.
Together we stand, hearts as one,
On bridges built, our lives begun.

Interwoven Dreams

In twilight's glow, our wishes form,
Threads of hope, a vibrant norm.
We stitch our dreams with silver light,
In every heart, a guiding sight.

With each soft breath, a tale unfolds,
A tapestry rich, with colors bold.
The fabric of life, in layers spun,
Interwoven paths, two become one.

Through gentle whispers, we create,
A world anew, where love is fate.
In quiet moments, where silence reigns,
Our dreams entwined, break all our chains.

As starlit skies begin to weave,
We hold the magic we believe.
In every heartbeat, a secret kept,
In dreams awash, our hopes adept.

With open arms, the night expands,
Together we rise, hands in hands.
Interwoven, forever we'll stay,
In this realm of dreams, come what may.

Lattices of Light

In the dawn's embrace, we find our way,
Lattices of light, shaping the day.
Each beam a promise, each shadow a sigh,
Crafting connections that never die.

Through storms we tread, and laughter's glow,
In every heart, a fire to stow.
Bound by the hope that binds us tight,
We dance along these paths of light.

With beams that ripple, we rise and fall,
In unity strong, we answer the call.
Through woven threads of bright delight,
Together we shine, in endless flight.

These lattices stretch, far and wide,
Guided by love, our constant guide.
In the vastness, we seek and find,
The radiant spark that lies intertwined.

So let the sunlight break through the night,
Together we bask in love's pure sight.
In this web of dreams, our souls ignite,
Forever bound in lattices of light.

Place Where Hearts Meet

Amidst the whispers of ancient trees,
A sacred ground, where spirits tease.
In every glance, a story starts,
In this cherished place, where hearts meet.

With kindness woven in each thread,
Where laughter blooms, and shadows shed.
Across the fields, where wildflowers sway,
Our souls entwined, come what may.

Through seasons change, we gather near,
In every joy, in every tear.
A sanctuary, where love takes flight,
In the stillness, we find our light.

As moonlight dances on our skin,
In the hush of night, our dreams begin.
Kaleidoscope visions, bright and sweet,
In this magical place, where hearts meet.

So let us linger, let us stay,
In this refuge, time melts away.
Together, always, in joy or defeat,
This is our haven, where hearts meet.

Synchronicity in Life

Moments align in a dance,
A glance, a chance, a glance,
Whispers from the universe,
Connecting us with subtle verse.

When paths converge, we find our way,
In signs and serendipity, we stay,
Each heartbeat synchronized with time,
A rhythm in life's seamless rhyme.

Fleeting hearts that beat as one,
Underneath the same bright sun,
A thread of fate weaves through the night,
Guiding us to shared delight.

In twinkling stars, we see our fate,
A tapestry we collaborate,
Together we breathe the same air,
In the chaos, we find the rare.

So let us dance on this great stage,
Embrace the magic, turn the page,
For in this symphony we reside,
Synchronicity as our guide.

Embracing the Unknown

In shadows cast by fears we hide,
Yet in the dark, the dreams reside,
A leap of faith, a whispered call,
To venture forth, beyond the fall.

Curious hearts seek what's concealed,
Through winding paths, our truths revealed,
With open arms, we face the night,
Embodying courage, seeking light.

Each twist and turn a brand new door,
Uncharted lands, we seek to explore,
With wonder as our faithful guide,
In uncertainty, we must abide.

The silence speaks in secret tones,
In the mystery, we find our own,
A canvas blank, awaiting strokes,
With every step, the fear provokes.

So take a breath and dive right in,
Embrace the unknown as your kin,
For life's a journey, brave and wide,
In the unknown, our souls confide.

Journeying Beyond

Beyond the hills and ocean blue,
A calling stirs, a dream anew,
With wanderlust as compass strong,
We march towards the great unknown.

Each mile unfolded like a tale,
Adventures wove through wind and sail,
With every step, the world expands,
New horizons stretch across the lands.

With eyes wide open, hearts alight,
We dance beneath the stars at night,
In whispers of the ancient trees,
We find the echoes of our dreams.

From snowy peaks to valleys deep,
In every silence, promises keep,
Embracing change, we find our way,
Journeying beyond, come what may.

So take my hand and let us roam,
For in this path, we find our home,
With spirits wild, we'll chase the sun,
Journeying together, always one.

The Shelter of Kinship

In gathered hearts, we find our rest,
With bonds that weave, we feel the best,
Through laughter shared and tears we shed,
In kinship's shelter, love is bred.

A shelter built of trust and grace,
In every hug, a warm embrace,
Together weathering the storm,
In our unity, forever warm.

Each story told, a thread we spin,
In our connection, we begin,
With open arms, we hold our fears,
In kinship's warmth, we dry the tears.

Through thick and thin, we're side by side,
In joy and sorrow, our hearts abide,
Creating memories that will last,
In the present, not the past.

So let us cherish this sacred bond,
For in our kinship, we'll respond,
With love that shines, a guiding star,
The shelter of kinship, near or far.

Affinity in Silence

In quiet nights, our hearts collide,
Words unspoken, love's gentle tide.
Eyes that meet, a world awakes,
In silence strong, the bond we make.

Hand in hand, no need for sound,
In stillness, deeper truths are found.
The whispering breeze, a soft embrace,
In tranquil moments, we find our place.

Through shadows cast, we forge the light,
A symphony in shades of night.
Each heartbeat echoes, forever near,
In affinity, there's naught to fear.

Lost in thoughts, yet time stands still,
Moments shared, we bend to will.
The language soft, a sacred dance,
In silence, we create our chance.

As dawn unfolds, our spirits soar,
In the hush, we crave for more.
Unraveled souls in tender flight,
Affinity thrives in quiet night.

Roots of Togetherness

In fertile ground, our roots entwined,
Nourished by love, so gentle, kind.
Shared dreams bloom, like flowers bright,
In harmony, we chase the light.

Through storms that shake the tallest tree,
Together strong, you stand by me.
Our laughter rings where shadows fall,
In unity, we conquer all.

With every season, we grow anew,
A tapestry woven in shades, so true.
Branches reaching for the sky,
In this embrace, we learn to fly.

When whispers fade, and troubles loom,
In depths of heart, we find the room.
Our strength, a bond that never breaks,
With roots of love, the earth awakes.

In moments shared, our legacy,
The echoes of sweet melody.
Bound together, forever blessed,
Roots of togetherness, our truest quest.

Nexus of the Divine

In sacred space, our spirits gleam,
Threads of purpose, woven dream.
Each tethered heart, a starlet hue,
In nexus bright, we find what's true.

Beyond the veil, we seek the grace,
In stillness blooms the holy place.
With whispered prayers, and timeless song,
In unity, where all belong.

Unseen forces, guiding light,
As shadows dance in day and night.
Our souls ignite, a timeless spark,
In the embrace of love's own arc.

Through sacred rites, and ancient lore,
In every heartbeat, we explore.
Together we rise, in faith we bind,
In the nexus, the divine we find.

Open your heart to the unseen flow,
In every challenge, together we grow.
In this embrace, our spirits dive,
In the nexus of the divine, we thrive.

Chords of the Spirit

In melodies soft, our souls entwine,
Chords of spirit, a sacred line.
With each note, our hearts align,
In symphony sweet, love's design.

The strum of life, both wild and bold,
In harmonies rich, our stories told.
Every heartbeat, a rhythmic play,
In the music, we find our way.

As echoes rise, the shadows fade,
With every chord, foundations laid.
We dance through trials, laughter's grace,
In the sound, we find our space.

Resonance deep, a bond so rare,
In the silence, we breathe the air.
With grateful hearts, the spirits sing,
In chords of love, forever spring.

So let the music weave and wind,
In every note, our hearts aligned.
Together we soar, in perfect tune,
Chords of the spirit, beneath the moon.

The Dance of Souls

In twilight's glow, two figures sway,
A gentle breeze guides their ballet.
Whispers of love, entwined in air,
Hearts move as one, no room for despair.

Step by step, they weave the night,
With every glance, igniting light.
A rhythm born from silent grace,
In this moment, time finds its place.

Beneath the stars, their shadows blend,
In an eternal waltz, no end.
Echoes of laughter, sweet and bright,
In the dance of souls, all feels right.

With every turn, the world fades away,
Lost in the music, they wish to stay.
Two hearts, one melody, pure and free,
Together forever, it's meant to be.

As dawn approaches, the dance slows down,
Yet in their hearts, they wear a crown.
For love, once sparked, will ever ignite,
In the dance of souls, they find their light.

Shadows of Affection

In corners dim, where whispers play,
Shadows of affection softly sway.
A tender touch, a gaze so deep,
In silent vows, their secrets keep.

Beneath the moon's soft, watchful eye,
Hearts exchange a low, sweet sigh.
Every gesture, a language made,
In the dusk, their fears allayed.

Footsteps echo in the night,
As warmth blossoms, pure delight.
A fleeting glance, a soft embrace,
Time stands still in this sacred space.

Their shadows dance, a fleeting dream,
Reflecting love's eternal theme.
In every heartbeat, every sigh,
The shadows whisper, never die.

Together they find solace there,
In each other's arms, none can compare.
For in the hours shared, they find,
The shadows of affection, intertwined.

Interwoven Dreams

In the tapestry of the night,
Two dreams emerge, bathed in light.
Threads of hope begin to weave,
In every heartbeat, they believe.

Stars align in a cosmic dance,
Every glance holds a hidden chance.
With every whisper, stories unfold,
Interwoven dreams, a treasure untold.

In quiet moments, while time stands still,
Hearts beat strongly, a gentle thrill.
A fabric rich with colors bright,
Drawn together, they feel the light.

Through challenges, they find their way,
In every dawn, love's bright bouquet.
Encouraged by the dreams they weave,
In each other, they choose to believe.

As night surrenders to the sun,
Two lives embrace, now as one.
A journey shared, forever gleams,
In the heart of interwoven dreams.

Celestial Embrace

Under a sky of endless blue,
Two souls converge, forever true.
Galaxies pulse, galaxies shine,
In each embrace, they redefine.

Soft as stardust, warm as the sun,
In their union, two worlds become one.
With every heartbeat, a cosmic song,
In celestial arms, they both belong.

Waves of love crash on the shore,
As they surrender, wanting more.
A universe crafted from whispers soft,
In the dance of light, they drift aloft.

Infinite skies, painted in dreams,
Love flows gently, or so it seems.
Every moment, an endless trace,
In the warmth of their celestial embrace.

When dusk falls and the stars ignite,
In that space, everything feels right.
Two souls entwined, forever they chase,
The boundless joy of a celestial embrace.

Resonance of Unity

In the garden where we stand,
Voices blend like grains of sand.
Every heart beats in accord,
Harmony our silent sword.

Through the storms we find our light,
Shining bright in darkest night.
Hand in hand, we rise anew,
Together strong, forever true.

Echoes dance upon the air,
Binding souls with tender care.
In the whispers, strength we find,
Uniting all, spirit entwined.

With every step upon this path,
We embrace joy and defy wrath.
The song of us, a mighty swell,
A tale of love we weave so well.

As the stars align above,
We nurture dreams and shared love.
Each moment we choose to share,
Is a promise, rich and rare.

The Rhythm of Together

In sync we move, a graceful dance,
Every glance, another chance.
Heartbeat echoes, one refrain,
In our rhythm, joy and pain.

Feet tapping on the crowded street,
Every stranger feels the beat.
A melody, soft and sweet,
Together we are incomplete.

With laughter bright and spirits high,
We reach for dreams beyond the sky.
United by the songs we sing,
In this bond, we find our wings.

With every note, our stories blend,
In harmony, we transcend.
Through trials, we find our grace,
In the dance, we find our place.

So let us journey hand in hand,
In every moment, take a stand.
With open hearts, we shall endeavor,
A rhythm strong, connecting forever.

Invisible Bonds

Threads of fate, unseen yet strong,
Weaving tales where we belong.
In the silence, whispers bind,
Invisible ties, hearts aligned.

Through every laugh and every tear,
These fragile threads connect us here.
A tapestry of dreams and fears,
Woven tight throughout the years.

Though miles apart, we feel it near,
An understanding, pure and clear.
In the shadows, love's embrace,
In every moment, we find grace.

Secret languages, shared with few,
We speak in colors, bright and true.
No distance can unravel fast,
Our invisible bonds, unsurpassed.

So hold on tight, for we are one,
In every shadow, every sun.
Together forged, forever tied,
In the dance of life, side by side.

Silken Threads of Fate

Silken threads that softly weave,
Stories only dreams conceive.
In the loom of life, we share,
Paths entwined with gentle care.

Each moment we touch, so divine,
In this fabric, your heart and mine.
Colors blending, rich and bold,
Tales of warmth and love retold.

With every stitch, a memory spun,
A treasure forged, two souls as one.
Through the needle's eye we find,
A journey vast, beautifully kind.

So let the world around us change,
While in this dance, we're free to range.
With every heartbeat, every breath,
We celebrate this bond, complex yet deft.

In the tapestry, our dreams ignite,
Silken threads gleaming in soft light.
Forever woven, hand in hand,
In love's embrace, forever stand.

A Chronicle of Belonging

In shadows cast by ancient trees,
We gather close, hearts at ease.
Each whispered tale, a sacred thread,
Binding us closer, where we tread.

Through laughter shared and tears we share,
In every moment, love laid bare.
We carve our names in time's embrace,
A testament to our warm space.

With every dawn, new dreams arise,
A tapestry stitched under bright skies.
In quiet places, our voices blend,
In this journey, we find no end.

Together we rise, together we fall,
In unity's strength, we conquer all.
Each heartbeat echoes, a lifelong song,
In this realm of belonging, we belong.

So let us walk, hand in hand,
Building our bond in this cherished land.
For every step through joy and strife,
Is a chapter written in the book of life.

Symphony of Companions

In harmony, we softly tread,
With hearts entwined, no words unsaid.
Each note a bond that we create,
In this symphony, we resonate.

Together we dance, under the stars,
With laughter and dreams, we heal our scars.
Through shifting tides, our spirits soar,
In this music, we are evermore.

From whispers shared on quiet nights,
To vibrant tales in morning light,
Each song we sing, a thread anew,
Bound by love, me and you.

In every struggle, we find our sound,
A resonance where trust is found.
In this life's orchestra, we play our role,
Each gentle refrain, a piece of soul.

So let the world hear our embrace,
In every chord, we find our place.
In this symphony, forever we'll be,
A melody of you, and a melody of me.

Unfolding the Spirit

In quiet moments, soft and deep,
Awakens the dreams we dare to keep.
With every breath, the soul expands,
A journey guided by unseen hands.

Through shadows dark, the light will break,
In every choice, the path we make.
With open hearts, we search for truth,
An endless quest, the bloom of youth.

In laughter's echo and silence' song,
The spirit whispers, guiding along.
In nature's arms, we find our peace,
Each moment lived, our worries cease.

In flowing rivers and mountains tall,
Nature unfolds, embracing all.
With every step, we learn to see,
The beauty held in simply being free.

So let us tread with gentle grace,
Unfolding spirits in this space.
Through every encounter, love ignites,
In the heart's deep glow, the spirit lights.

Cloak of Kinship

Worn softly like a cherished thread,
The cloak of kinship wraps our head.
In every fold, a story's spun,
Of lives entwined, two becoming one.

Through laughter's warmth and tears so bright,
We share the burdens of the night.
Within its weave, a bond we find,
Crafting moments, heart intertwined.

In times of joy and times of pain,
This cloak will shelter, keep us sane.
In every stitch, a memory gleams,
A fabric woven with hopeful dreams.

As seasons change and years drift by,
We wear our cloak beneath the sky.
In each embrace, we find our grace,
With kinship's love, we carve our place.

So let the world see our embrace,
In every challenge, we find our pace.
The cloak of kinship, strong and true,
Wraps us tight, me and you.

Unbroken Circles

In quiet moments, we convene,
The echoes linger, softly seen.
Bound by threads, both old and new,
Unbroken circles, tried and true.

Through seasons shifting, hearts remain,
A bond that time cannot contain.
In laughter's light, in shadows tall,
Together rise, together fall.

With every step, our spirits soar,
In unity, we seek for more.
The dance of life, a sacred ring,
In harmony, our souls take wing.

When storms may come, with raging fire,
We find in each, a calm desire.
To hold each other, true and fast,
Unbroken circles, unsurpassed.

In memories, the warmth resides,
A timeless love that never hides.
Through whispered vows, we write our story,
In each embrace, a tale of glory.

In twilight's glow, we stand as one,
Our journey's end, just but begun.
Unbroken whispers in the night,
Together bound, we embrace the light.

Intangible Affinities

Across the cosmos, a silent thread,
Connecting hearts, where dreams are fed.
In a glance shared, emotions flow,
Intangible ties that softly grow.

In shadows cast by stars above,
We find the pulse of endless love.
Through whispered sighs and gentle grace,
Our souls entwine in sacred space.

With every heartbeat, a story forged,
In quiet realms where hopes surged.
Where distance fails, our spirits meet,
Intangible affinities, so sweet.

When laughter rings, when silence sighs,
A dance of souls beneath the skies.
In colors bright and shades of grey,
We chase the dawn, we greet the day.

Time may drift, as rivers flow,
Yet here we stand, through ebb and glow.
In every moment, we recall,
Intangible bonds that hold us all.

The Dance of Kindred

In twilight's embrace, we find our place,
The dance of kindred, a sweet grace.
With hands held tight, we spin and sway,
Under the moon's soft silver ray.

With laughter light, and voices clear,
We celebrate all that we hold dear.
Each twirl a promise, each step a vow,
In sacred rhythm, we live in now.

Through seasons turning, we find delight,
In every shadow, a spark of light.
Hearts that mirror, in joy and strife,
The dance of kindred, the pulse of life.

With open arms, we welcome fate,
In this grand dance, we elevate.
Through trials faced and dreams embraced,
We weave a tale that won't be erased.

The music plays, and we respond,
In every heartbeat, we dare to bond.
Together we sway, in perfect time,
The dance of kindred, forever sublime.

Guardians of the Soul

In silent whispers, we stand tall,
Guardians of the soul, we hear the call.
In shadows deep, we find our way,
Through storms of doubt, we choose to stay.

With steadfast hearts, we brave the night,
Together facing what feels right.
In every tear, in every smile,
We share the journey, mile by mile.

Through the tangled paths of fate,
We weave our dreams, we cultivate.
With gentle strength, we rise anew,
Guardians true, for me and you.

In every challenge, bold we stand,
Bound by love's ever-quiet hand.
With open hearts, we share our role,
As faithful watchers of the soul.

In twilight's glow, we find our peace,
A sacred bond that will not cease.
Guardians of the heart's embrace,
Together forever, we hold our place.

Haven of Heartstrings

In a garden where shadows play,
Soft whispers of love drift away.
The petals sway in gentle breeze,
A sanctuary where hearts find ease.

Moonlight dances on the grass,
Time slows down, moments amass.
With every sigh and sweet caress,
This haven, a tender recess.

Gentle hands, a guiding touch,
In your presence, I feel so much.
Beneath the stars, our dreams ignite,
Love's lullaby sings in the night.

When the world feels cold and gray,
Your laughter warms, chasing dismay.
Through storms, our spirits intertwine,
A safe space where our souls align.

Here in this place, so serene,
We weave our story, like a dream.
With every heartbeat, ever near,
Our haven of heartstrings draws us here.

Eternal Embrace

In twilight's glow, we stand so still,
Two souls entwined, unbreakable will.
The universe sings our silent song,
In this love, we both belong.

Time may stretch, then swiftly fly,
Yet in your gaze, my hopes comply.
A world anew through every glance,
In your arms, I take a chance.

With threads of silver, fate we spin,
Each whisper wraps where love begins.
In every heartbeat, echoes trace,
The warmth of our eternal embrace.

Let shadows fall, let tempests roam,
In your love, I've found my home.
Together we shine, a radiant light,
Guided by stars, through the night.

This moment lingers, forever drawn,
In the dawn, our spirits yawn.
Embraced in dreams, we rise and soar,
In love, we are forever more.

Interlaced Journeys

Paths entwined beneath the sky,
Two souls journeying, you and I.
With every step, our story grows,
In whispered secrets, affection flows.

Mountains high and rivers wide,
Onward we roam, side by side.
Each winding road, a tale unfolds,
In the warmth of hands we hold.

Through valleys deep, through storms we tread,
In laughter's light, our worries shed.
In solace found along the way,
Together we face the light of day.

Stars may shift, and seasons change,
Yet with you, nothing feels strange.
Interlaced dreams set our course,
In this journey, love's our force.

As sunsets paint the sky in gold,
Our hearts, a map, a future bold.
With each horizon, fresh and bright,
Our paths converge, we take flight.

The Lattice of Us

In the fabric of life, we weave our fate,
Threads of laughter, a tapestry great.
Colors of joy in vibrant hues,
The lattice of us, a bond we choose.

Through seasons' change and trials faced,
In every stitch, our love is laced.
Moments stitched with care and grace,
In this lattice, we find our place.

The patterns shift, yet still remain,
A dance of hearts in love's refrain.
Together we build, together we stand,
In this lattice, hand in hand.

Each knot a memory, strong and true,
Binding us close, just me and you.
In woven dreams, we find our trust,
A sanctuary built, the lattice of us.

As time unfolds with gentle ease,
Our hearts entwined like swaying trees.
Rooted deeply, we grow as one,
In the lattice of love, we have begun.

Home in Each Other

In your eyes, I find my peace,
A warmth that never seems to cease.
Together we build our dreams,
In a world that softly gleams.

Through storms and trials, hand in hand,
We navigate this promised land.
With whispered laugh and shared sigh,
Our hearts, like stars, will ever fly.

In every challenge, we stand tall,
Together we'll conquer it all.
A sanctuary, a gentle embrace,
Our love, a never-ending space.

Where laughter echoes through the night,
And shadows fade to purest light.
In the silence, our souls take flight,
Home in each other feels so right.

With every moment, time stands still,
In your presence, I find my thrill.
Together, we'll face what's to come,
In this love, we are truly home.

Starlit Entwining

Under the sky, where dreams reside,
We dance together, hearts open wide.
With whispers soft as evening's breath,
In starlit nights, we find our depth.

Your hand in mine, a perfect fit,
As constellations around us flit.
We weave our tales in cosmic curls,
Entwined forever, boy and girl.

The moon leads us on paths unknown,
In this vast universe, we have grown.
With every glance, our spirits soar,
Bound by the stars, we seek more.

Our laughter mingles with the night,
Creating magic, pure delight.
As galaxies witness our warm embrace,
We find our world in this sacred space.

Together we drift on dreams so bright,
Guided by love, our endless light.
In starlit skies, forever free,
In each other, our destiny.

Circles of Influences

In gentle waves, we sway and spin,
Life's rhythm leads us, drawing in.
Each person placed along our paths,
Creates the story in the aftermath.

With every smile that we bestow,
A ripple spreads, a chance to grow.
Like rings in water, spreading wide,
Each connection is a source of pride.

Through joy and sorrow, share the tears,
With open hearts, we ease our fears.
In circles small, or circles grand,
The threads of fate tie hand in hand.

We weave our dreams, entwined as one,
In every battle, battles won.
From whispers soft to echoes strong,
Together we form the perfect song.

Through every life, our footprints trace,
Leaving a mark, a warm embrace.
In the circles formed, we find our place,
Influences bloom in love's sweet grace.

Connections Like Rivers

As rivers flow, so do our hearts,
Each twist and turn, a brand new start.
With every drop, a story told,
In the currents, memories unfold.

We rush through valleys, wide and deep,
In tranquil pools, our secrets keep.
Together we carve through solid stone,
Each bend reveals how we've grown.

With laughter ringing through the air,
And gentle whispers, soft and rare,
Like rivers meeting, we connect,
In flowing streams, we share respect.

Our waters merge beneath the skies,
Creating beauty that never dies.
Through seasons, ebbing, flowing wide,
In every current, we abide.

Together we journey, hand in hand,
Through every river, every strand.
In connections strong, our souls entwine,
Like rivers flowing, forever shine.

Resonating Echoes

In the valley where whispers play,
Echoes of laughter drift away.
Songs of the past in the breeze blow,
Memories linger, soft and slow.

Time flows like a gentle stream,
Carrying wishes, weaving a dream.
In the twilight, shadows dance light,
Fading softly into the night.

Footsteps crunch on a path well-trod,
Each step, a story, a silent nod.
Nature's chorus sings along,
Crafting the notes of an unwritten song.

Hearts entwined like vines that climb,
Over fences, through spaces, in rhyme.
In each echo, a part of their sound,
Love resounding, forever profound.

As the stars peek through the sky,
The resonance of dreams does not die.
In every heartbeat, in every sigh,
Resonating echoes will always fly.

Intertwined Destinies

In the tapestry of this life we weave,
Threads of fates that never deceive.
Two souls dancing, in sync they sway,
Bound together, come what may.

Paths that cross like rivers flow,
Each current brings a brand new show.
Through the storms and bright weather,
The thread unites, now and forever.

Dreams whispered softly in the dark,
Igniting hope with a gentle spark.
In every glance, a promise shines,
Weaving futures on delicate lines.

Hands entwined, they face the dawn,
Together strong, never withdrawn.
With shared laughter and echoing cries,
Intertwined destinies, under the skies.

Time will stretch, and seasons change,
Yet their bond will never rearrange.
In every heartbeat, they find their way,
Intertwined destinies, here to stay.

Beneath Shared Stars

Under a canopy of shimmering night,
Two souls meet, hearts taking flight.
Beneath the stars, their dreams align,
In this moment, the worlds combine.

Soft whispers float in the midnight air,
Promises made without a care.
Hand in hand, they chase the light,
Lost in the magic of the night.

Every twinkle tells a story old,
Secrets of love and wishes bold.
In the silence, their hopes ignite,
Beneath shared stars, everything feels right.

With every glance, they find their grace,
In the universe, they've found their place.
Together they dance, hearts aglow,
In the glow of the celestial show.

As dawn's light begins to break,
They hold the dreams that they both make.
Through every moment, near or far,
Their love shines bright, beneath the stars.

Enigma of Togetherness

In the silence where feelings bloom,
An enigma breathes, dispelling gloom.
Two hearts beat in a sacred place,
Searching for trust and a warm embrace.

Unraveled paths woven tight,
Tracing shadows, chasing light.
In the space where souls collide,
An unspoken bond, a secret guide.

Through trials faced, their spirits rise,
Embracing the truth, beyond disguise.
In tangled moments, they find their way,
The enigma of togetherness guides their stay.

With whispered hopes and tender dreams,
Life's complex web is not as it seems.
In the mysteries held by the heart,
Together, never shall they part.

In laughter shared and tears released,
They find solace, love's pure feast.
Amidst the chaos, they softly confess,
The enigma of togetherness, their true success.

The Unseen Symphony

In whispers soft, the notes arise,
They dance on air beneath the skies.
Each chord a heartbeat, pulsing free,
An unseen tune, a mystery.

The rustling leaves, they sway and sway,
A melody of night and day.
With every breeze, the music flows,
In silence deep, the symphony grows.

Stars twinkle in the velvet dark,
Each shine a note, a hidden spark.
The moon conducts with silver light,
Guiding dreams through endless night.

Feel the rhythm in the soul,
Life's gentle song, it makes us whole.
In quiet corners, the echoes play,
An unseen hymn that finds its way.

So listen close, and you might find,
A harmony that binds mankind.
In every heart, a song resides,
The unseen symphony abides.

Weaving Dreams Together

Threads of hope, entwined with care,
In the loom of night, our dreams we share.
With every stitch, a tale is spun,
A tapestry of all we've won.

Colors burst in every hue,
A vibrant world, both old and new.
Woven stories, soft yet strong,
In this fabric, we belong.

The whispers of the past remain,
In every knot, a joy, a pain.
Together we bind, never apart,
Weaving dreams with all our heart.

Patterns form as we unite,
Through shared visions, we ignite.
In every thread, a soul laid bare,
Connected, held in love and care.

With each new dawn, our dreams will grow,
In the loom of life, our spirits flow.
Together, stronger, hearts in tether,
We are the weavers, forever together.

Guardians of Heritage

In echoes deep, the stories lie,
Guardians watch as seasons pass by.
With ancient roots, we stand and stay,
Preserving past in every way.

Traditions woven in the clay,
In every heart, they find their way.
Through songs and tales, we keep them bright,
Guardians of heritage, our guiding light.

Through time's embrace, we carry forth,
The wisdom of those who walked before.
In every heartbeat, in every breath,
We honor life, we honor death.

With hands held high, we celebrate,
The threads of culture we elevate.
In unity, we find our grace,
Guardians of heritage, we hold our place.

As new tales rise with every dawn,
We weave the past in moments gone.
Together we stand, united and free,
Guardians of all that is legacy.

Threads of Memory

In shadows cast by fading light,
Threads of memory take their flight.
Each moment lingers, sweet and clear,
A tapestry of love held dear.

Stitches of joy and tales of tears,
Woven together through the years.
In every thread, a story spun,
A life well lived, a race well run.

Fleeting whispers of days gone by,
In silent corners, they softly lie.
Captured in threads of golden hue,
Every memory, a piece of you.

As time unravels, we hold it tight,
The threads of memory shine so bright.
Through laughter and pain, we find our way,
In woven tales that never fray.

So let us cherish, let us bind,
Threads of memory intertwined.
In every smile, in every tear,
A cherished past forever near.

The Language of Kin

In whispered tones and knowing glances,
A bond that grows with every chance.
Echoes of laughter, stories shared,
In the heart's chambers, love is declared.

Roots entwined in sun and rain,
Through every joy, through every pain.
Silent gestures, a touch, a sigh,
In the language of kin, we never say goodbye.

Through seasons change, we stand as one,
In the setting moon, in the rising sun.
For every heartbeat in the night,
Our spirits dance in endless light.

Moments caught in time's embrace,
In the arms of kin, we find our place.
A tapestry woven with threads of gold,
In every memory, stories unfold.

Together we'll climb, together we'll fall,
In the language of kin, we hear the call.
No distance strong, no time too late,
In the bonds of love, we celebrate.

Pathways of Affection

Through winding trails where shadows play,
In the garden of hearts, we find our way.
Hands held tight in the softening dusk,
In glances exchanged, there lies a trust.

Footsteps echo on the cobblestone,
In silence we speak, never alone.
Moments drift like leaves in the breeze,
In the warmth of love, we find our ease.

Every whisper like a gentle song,
In pathways of affection, we belong.
With every sunrise, new hopes arise,
In your presence, my spirit flies.

Through valleys deep and mountains high,
In every laughter, we touch the sky.
Together we wander, hand in hand,
In the fabric of love, we make our stand.

As stars illuminate the night's soft hue,
In the heart's compass, there lies the true.
Through every season, our love persists,
In pathways of affection, we coexist.

Timeless Embrace

In the stillness of the evening's glow,
Whispers of love begin to flow.
In each gentle caress, a story is told,
In the warmth of your arms, I'm never cold.

Time stands still when I hold you near,
In every heartbeat, I feel no fear.
Through the dance of shadows and light,
In our timeless embrace, everything feels right.

With every breath, our souls entwine,
In the tapestry of love, the threads align.
Moments eternal, they stretch and blend,
In the cradle of time, we find no end.

Through life's storms, we stand as one,
In silence and laughter, two become one.
A symphony played in the softest of sighs,
In the depths of your gaze, the universe lies.

In every memory, in every trace,
There's beauty and joy in our timeless embrace.
Forever we'll dance under stars above,
In the essence of life, we find our love.

Echoing Heartbeats

In the quiet moments where shadows blend,
Our heartbeat echoes, the sound of a friend.
With every rhythm, a story unfolds,
In the depths of silence, a truth to be told.

Through the laughter and whispers, we share our dreams,
In the fabric of life, love's thread gleams.
Every heartbeat a promise, steadfast and dear,
In the symphony of life, you're always near.

As stars twinkle in the vast night sky,
In the canvas of time, we breathe, we fly.
With each echo, our spirits unite,
In this dance of existence, we ignite.

Through the changes and trials that life may send,
In the echoes we find, we begin, we mend.
Resonating softly, our hearts sing the tune,
In the presence of love, we swoon.

Together we journey through time's gentle bend,
In the echoing heartbeats, we find our blend.
A tapestry woven, forever will stay,
In the echoes of love, we'll find our way.

Heart's Cartography

Paths we tread, with gentle heart,
Mapping love, a sacred art.
In every beat, a trace remains,
Guiding us through joy and pains.

Whispers soft, through shadows creep,
In the silence, promises keep.
Each turn leads to vast unknown,
In the journey, seeds are sown.

Markers placed in tender smile,
Every moment, worth the while.
Through valleys deep, on mountains high,
Together we will reach the sky.

With every map, a story told,
Of warmth and courage, brave and bold.
In every heart, a compass beats,
Navigating what love meets.

Join me now, let's pave the way,
In our hearts, forever stay.
Together drawing every line,
In heart's cartography, you are mine.

The Pulse of Fellowship

In laughter shared, the pulse runs free,
A bond that thrives, just you and me.
Through trials faced, in storms we stand,
Together strong, a steady hand.

Echoes of joy in every cheer,
In silent moments, we draw near.
The warmth of friendship, softly glows,
Through every storm, the heart knows.

In every tear, a shared embrace,
In every triumph, we find our grace.
A rhythm that unites our souls,
Fellowship makes the fractured whole.

Through paths of light and shadows cast,
With every heartbeat, friendships last.
In unity, we build our dreams,
A tapestry of vibrant themes.

So gather close, let spirits rise,
In fellowship, our love defies.
Together we will face the days,
In the pulse of life, love always stays.

Uncharted Affinities

In fleeting glances, sparks ignite,
A dance of souls, both day and night.
The call of fate, so sweet, so rare,
Uncharted paths, with hearts laid bare.

With every word, a thread we weave,
In whispered dreams, we dare believe.
The unknown waits, with arms extended,
In this new world, our hearts suspended.

Through winding ways, we wander true,
In this vast realm, just me and you.
Each moment shared, a treasure trove,
In uncharted lands, our spirits rove.

With every step, we learn, we grow,
Through laughter's light and sorrow's flow.
In affinities that break the mold,
New stories waiting to be told.

So take my hand, let's chart the skies,
In uncharted realms, our spirits rise.
Together we'll find what love can be,
In mystery's embrace, just you and me.

Bonds of the Heart

In tender moments, our spirits tie,
Bonds of the heart that never die.
Through laughter's light and sorrow's veil,
Together we will find the trail.

Each whispered word, a promise made,
A sanctuary where love won't fade.
In every touch, a language clear,
With bonds of the heart, we banish fear.

Through storms that rage and skies that weep,
In quiet hours, our love runs deep.
We stand united, both strong and free,
In this sacred space, just you and me.

Threads of connection, bold and bright,
In darkest times, you are my light.
With every heartbeat, ties renew,
In bonds of the heart, love always true.

So let us dance through years untold,
In warmth and joy, our love unfolds.
With every moment, let it impart,
The endless strength of bonds of heart.

Threads of the Eternal

In shadows deep, the ancients weave,
A tapestry of time, we believe.
Each thread a story, softly spun,
In the loom of life, we are one.

Whispers echo through the night,
Guiding souls with gentle light.
Across the ages, our hearts align,
In this dance, our fates entwine.

Stars above, like dreams, they shine,
Reminding us of love's design.
Each moment passed, a stitch refined,
In the fabric of the divine.

Through trials faced, our spirits grow,
The strength of bonds we come to know.
With every heartbeat, every sigh,
The threads of fate, we cannot deny.

So let us cherish what we hold,
The tales of life, both brave and bold.
For in this journey, we are pure,
Eternal threads that will endure.

Bonds Woven by Destiny

Two souls meet under a vast expanse,
A fleeting moment, a steadfast glance.
In the tapestry of fate, they entwine,
Creating bonds, through love divine.

Across time's river, they gently flow,
With every heartbeat, their spirits grow.
In laughter's echo and tears' embrace,
Destiny guides with a perfect grace.

Through trials faced and joys shared,
With open hearts and souls laid bare.
Each thread a promise, each knot a vow,
Together they stand, in the now.

The fabric woven, thread by thread,
In every word, in silence said.
An eternal bond, strong and true,
In the heart's design, just me and you.

So let the stars bear witness bright,
To the love that fills the night.
With every breath, we forge anew,
Bonds woven tight, forever true.

Whispered Connections

In quiet corners, secrets dwell,
With whispers soft, they weave a spell.
In every glance, a world unfolds,
With stories shared and dreams retold.

The gentle breeze carries our sighs,
Underneath the wide, open skies.
With every heartbeat, we draw near,
In whispered tones, our souls appear.

Embracing hope in the stillness found,
A melody sweet, in silence bound.
The threads of fate connect our souls,
In this vast journey, we are whole.

With laughter bright and tears that flow,
In moments shared, we come to know.
That every path, though long and wide,
Leads us back to love's soft side.

So hold these whispers, soft and dear,
In connection forged, we have no fear.
For in this dance, we find our place,
Whispered connections, love's embrace.

Embrace of the Ancients

In shadows of old, the ancients stand,
Guardians of time, with a steady hand.
Their whispers echo in rustling leaves,
In their embrace, the heart believes.

Through winding paths, their wisdom flows,
In the heart's journey, true love knows.
With every step, their presence felt,
In silent moments, our spirits melt.

The stars above, a guiding light,
Illuminating paths through the night.
In the embrace of stories spun,
Our souls awaken, become as one.

Through trials faced, they lend their might,
In dreams woven, they take flight.
A legacy rich, a bond so strong,
In the embrace of the ancients, we belong.

So let us gather 'neath ancient trees,
In their arms, find comfort and ease.
For in this bond, we shall remain,
In the embrace of the ancients, love's refrain.

Embracing the Unseen

In shadows where the whispers lie,
A dance of dreams that reach the sky.
They flicker softly, barely there,
Yet weave a tapestry of care.

In silence, secrets gently play,
Guiding hearts in their array.
A fleeting touch, a fleeting glance,
Inviting souls to take a chance.

The unseen paths, a winding trail,
Through winds of doubt, they never pale.
With every breath, we choose to see,
The beauty stitched in mystery.

For in the void, we find our song,
Where all the lost notes do belong.
Embracing joys we rarely greet,
In shadows deep, our hearts compete.

A gentle nudge, a silent cheer,
In unseen realms, love draws us near.
Together strong, we rise, we soar,
Embracing what's just beyond the door.

Harmony in Heartstrings

A melody played in tender truth,
Echoes of love in the bloom of youth.
Together we dance on notes so bright,
Creating the harmony that feels just right.

Serenades sung in the quiet night,
Two souls entwined, hearts taking flight.
With every pulse, our rhythms blend,
Crafting a song that will never end.

In laughter and tears, our spirits sing,
Creating a world where hope can cling.
With every chord, we find a way,
To stay together, come what may.

The strings are taut, the tension high,
Yet in each note, a reason why.
Through every storm and gentle breeze,
We strum the heartstrings to find our ease.

So let us play this timeless tune,
Under stars and the watchful moon.
Together in rhythm, forever we'll be,
In harmony, just you and me.

Woven Legacies

Threads of stories, intertwined,
Each moment captured, brilliantly aligned.
The fabric of time, rich and bold,
A tapestry of memories told.

In every stitch, a life unfolds,
Of laughter, love, and dreams of gold.
Communities built on the strength of hope,
A legacy woven, teaching us to cope.

From generations past, wisdom flows,
In the heart of every child, it grows.
With threads of courage and vibrant hues,
Our shared heritage, a love so true.

The loom of life spins ever on,
A masterpiece waiting to be drawn.
With hands that guide, we create our fate,
In the quiet moments, we resonate.

So cherish the threads that bind us tight,
A woven legacy, our guiding light.
In every heart, a piece remains,
A testament to love that sustains.

Eternal Knots

Ties that bind, unseen yet strong,
In the tapestry of life, we all belong.
With every knot, a story shared,
In the journey of love, truly prepared.

Through trials faced and bridges crossed,
In the web of time, we count no cost.
For every challenge, a bond grows tight,
In the starlit sky, we find our light.

No force can sever what's intertwined,
In moments fleeting, our spirits aligned.
Each knot a promise, a vow we keep,
In the heart's embrace, our dreams run deep.

Bound by trust, we rise, we fall,
Yet through it all, we stand tall.
Eternal knots, our anchor, our guide,
Together forever, side by side.

So let us cherish what we entwine,
In the fabric of life, our hearts combine.
With every thread, our bond entwines,
In the dance of time, true love defines.

Unity in Diversity

In colors bright, we stand as one,
Different paths, but journeys begun.
Our voices blend, a chorus free,
Together we grow, in harmony.

Each story told, a vibrant thread,
Weaving life where shadows tread.
In myriad hearts, a common beat,
United we rise, no retreat.

Through choices made, and hands we share,
A tapestry rich, beyond compare.
Embracing strengths, we lift each other,
In unity found, like sister and brother.

From varied roots, our branches soar,
Nurtured by love, forever more.
Let differences shine, a radiant spark,
In the tapestry woven, we leave our mark.

Together we stand, with courage's flame,
In this dance of life, no one's to blame.
Diversity blooms, an endless sea,
In unity's grasp, we all are free.

Connection in Stillness

In whispers soft, the world unfolds,
In quiet moments, the heart consoled.
Beneath the stars, our souls align,
In stillness found, a spark divine.

The gentle breeze, a tender touch,
Reminds us all, we're loved so much.
In silent gaze, a bond so deep,
In tranquil waters, our spirits leap.

Disconnect the noise, let chaos fade,
In present stillness, a peace is laid.
We find our truth in moments rare,
In connection's grace, we breathe the air.

Through mindful breaths, we draw in light,
In soft embrace, we know what's right.
In stillness shared, we find our way,
In sacred whispers, we choose to stay.

Together we sit, hand in hand,
In silence profound, we make our stand.
The world outside may whirl and spin,
But in this stillness, our hearts begin.

The Heart's Mosaic

Fragments scattered, yet whole we weave,
Each piece a story that we believe.
In every heart, a unique design,
Together they shine, a spark divine.

In laughter bright or shadows cast,
Memories woven that hold us fast.
Through joyful tears and whispered dreams,
The heart's mosaic, or so it seems.

With colors bold, and shades of grey,
Each moment passed lights up the way.
In unity found, our spirits dance,
With every beat, we take a chance.

The bits we gather, a treasure chest,
Celebrating life, in every quest.
For in this masterpiece, every part,
Every puzzle fits, inside the heart.

Our tales entwined, in life's embrace,
Through trials faced, we find our place.
In vibrant shards, together we mend,
The heart's mosaic, with love to send.

Enchanted Links

In twilight's hush, connections bloom,
With every glance, dispelling gloom.
Through laughter shared and stories spun,
The bonds we form, two become one.

In whispered dreams, our spirits rise,
With every heartbeat, beneath the skies.
Through tangled paths, we journey far,
As enchanted links, we are the stars.

With hands entwined, we navigate,
Through joy and sorrow, we celebrate.
Each moment cherished, a radiant thread,
In woven memories, love and hope spread.

From souls ignited, to hearts aflame,
In every echo, we call each name.
With strength we build, in trust we grow,
Through enchanted links, our spirits flow.

Together we shine, a brilliant light,
In every challenge, we find our might.
For in these links, we're never alone,
In memories crafted, our love has grown.

Threads of Connection

In the quiet moments, we find,
Woven paths that twist and bind.
Softly shared, our hearts align,
Threads of connection, strong, refined.

Every story, every glance,
Carries echoes of our dance.
In the fabric, dreams enhance,
Tapestry of shared romance.

Miles may stretch, yet still unite,
Through the dark, we seek the light.
Invisible strings hold us tight,
In the silence, love takes flight.

With every laugh and tear we sow,
Roots intertwine, beginnings grow.
Through seasons change, we come to know,
Threads of connection softly flow.

In the warmth of tender ties,
Hope and fear flash like the skies.
With every heartbeat, love replies,
Threads of connection never die.

Whispers in the Roots

Deep within the earth they lie,
Whispers bloom where secrets sigh.
Beneath the surface, life's embrace,
Roots entwined in timeless space.

Softly spoken words of old,
In the silence, stories told.
Life's foundation, strong and bold,
Whispers in the roots unfold.

Tangled journeys we descend,
Through the soil, we weave and mend.
In nature's arms, we find a friend,
Whispers in the roots, they blend.

Growth and strength emerge in trust,
From the past, we rise from dust.
With every heartbeat, in us thrust,
Whispers in the roots, a must.

Through all seasons, we bear witness,
Nature's lore in quiet fitness.
In this life, we find our business,
Whispers in the roots, our richness.

Weaving Bonds of Old

In the twilight, shadows gather,
Echoes of a time that lather.
Crafted tales in threads of gold,
Weaving bonds that never fold.

Memories held with gentle hands,
In the heart, a love that stands.
Two souls dancing in the night,
Weaving bonds, pure and bright.

With each stitch, we trace the past,
Moments cherished, meant to last.
Through laughter, joy, and sweet despair,
Weaving bonds, a loving pair.

Tales of struggle, joy, and fate,
Stories woven, never late.
In the fabric, voices call,
Weaving bonds to bridge it all.

Hand in hand, we forge our way,
In the night, we find our play.
Through every weave, come what may,
Weaving bonds of love today.

Celestial Threads

Stars above begin to gleam,
Weaving dreams into the stream.
Night unfolds with gentle grace,
Celestial threads in time and space.

Galaxies spin in whispered tunes,
Painting skies with silver dunes.
In the cosmos, we ascend,
Celestial threads that never end.

Each light a spark, a journey's tale,
Across the void, our spirits sail.
Through stardust paths, we transcend,
Celestial threads our hearts commend.

In the silence, cosmic sighs,
Echoes of our love arise.
Woven tight, the universe cries,
Celestial threads, where hope lies.

Together we dance among the stars,
Hearts aligned, erased the scars.
In this night, love truly bled,
Celestial threads that we have wed.

Guardians of The Heart

In shadows deep, where secrets hide,
The guardians stand, side by side.
They shield the dreams from piercing woes,
With whispers soft, the love they chose.

Through storms that rage and tempests roar,
They hold their ground, forevermore.
A bond unbroken, fierce and true,
In every heartbeat, they renew.

Their watchful eyes, like stars afar,
Illuminate paths, no matter how far.
With tender strength, they guide the way,
Through darkest nights, to light of day.

In laughter shared and tears that fall,
The guardians rise, they never stall.
Each chapter written, tales unfold,
In the book of hearts, their love is gold.

For every wound and every scar,
They mend with grace, like gentle spar.
In silence loud, their hearts do sing,
As guardians of love, they bring spring.

Beneath the Same Sky

Two souls afar, yet close at heart,
Beneath the same sky, they're never apart.
With every star, a wish is made,
In the tapestry of night, love is laid.

Through whispered winds, their secrets flow,
A bond unseen, that continues to grow.
In every dawn, in every dusk,
Their hearts entwined in endless trust.

They share the moon in silver light,
Guiding dreams through tranquil night.
With each heartbeat, they softly sigh,
Floating on love, they learn to fly.

Across the miles, a journey wide,
Together they stand, with hearts as guide.
No distance strong, no mountains high,
For love transcends beneath the sky.

Together they find hope and grace,
In every moment, they embrace.
For though apart, they feel the tune,
Of love that dances under the moon.

The Covenant of Souls

In a sacred pact, their spirits bind,
The covenant of souls, forever entwined.
Through trials faced and moments shared,
A promise made, a love declared.

With every sunset, a vow renewed,
In silent whispers, deep and true.
Together they rise, together they fall,
In the heart's embrace, they give their all.

They walk the path, hand in hand,
In life's vast sea, they make their stand.
Through storms that bruise and winds that wail,
Their love remains, a steadfast sail.

In every heartbeat, a gentle song,
A reminder that they truly belong.
Through lifetimes past, their journey flows,
In the covenant of souls, love always grows.

With each new dawn and twilight's call,
Their spirits soar, they will not fall.
For in this bond, they find their way,
Infinite love, come what may.

Weaving the Unseen

In threads of time, they start to weave,
A tapestry of dreams, they believe.
With colors bright, and shadows cast,
They stitch the moments, hold them fast.

Each strand a story, rich and bold,
Of joy and sorrow, life unfolds.
With careful hands, they craft with care,
An unseen bond, forever rare.

Through laughter light and tears that flow,
They weave the unseen, letting love grow.
In every knot, a wish is tied,
In every loop, their hearts confide.

As patterns form in intricate grace,
They find their peace in this sacred space.
In the warmth of love, they softly dream,
Weaving the unseen, a flowing stream.

With every dawn, a new design,
Together they flourish, your heart in mine.
In life's grand loom, their tales align,
Weaving the unseen, forever divine.

Threads of Destiny

In the fabric of night, we weave our dreams,
Threads intertwine like shimmering beams.
Each choice a stitch, a fate defined,
In the tapestry of time, our hearts aligned.

With gentle hands, we pull each thread,
Colors of hope where shadows tread.
Moments entwined in a symphony sweet,
Guided by whispers, our souls shall meet.

Through valleys deep and mountains high,
We chase the stars in the endless sky.
No path is straight, nor journey brief,
Yet in every turn, we find belief.

With every twist and every turn,
Lessons of life are what we learn.
In the loom of fate, together we stand,
Crafting our futures, hand in hand.

So let us not fear what lies ahead,
For destiny calls with words unsaid.
With courage bold, we'll take the chance,
To dance through the night in life's expanse.

Bridges of Belonging

Across the waters, we build our way,
Bridges of hope that never sway.
With every plank, a story shared,
In the hearts of many, love declared.

Through storms and trials, we stand as one,
Together we rise, like the morning sun.
Each step we take, a promise made,
In the circle of life, we're never afraid.

The laughter echoes, the tears we shed,
In moments of joy, in words unsaid.
We gather close; we draw the line,
In the warmth of kinship, we always shine.

With hands wide open and hearts so true,
We break down walls and see it through.
United in purpose, forever strong,
Through the bridges of belonging, we all belong.

Let every heartbeat connect us deep,
In this bond of trust, our dreams we keep.
Together we'll thrive, together we'll sing,
For in this unity, our spirits take wing.

Unbreakable Links

In the chain of life, we find our place,
Links of connection, filled with grace.
Stronger together, we stand as one,
In the dance of time, our journey begun.

Through trials and joys, we hold on tight,
In the darkest hours, we find the light.
With laughter and tears, we pave the way,
In the warmth of love, we choose to stay.

Each bond we forge, a story unfolds,
In whispers of fate, our hearts are bold.
With steady hands and fearless hearts,
We cherish the ties that never depart.

In moments of doubt, we raise our voice,
In unity found, we make our choice.
For every link forms a part of the whole,
In the unbreakable chain, we find our soul.

Through seasons of change, our spirit will gleam,
In the tapestry woven, we dare to dream.
Together we rise, together we sing,
In the bonds of love, we find our wings.

Voices in the Silence

In the stillness, whispers dance,
Echoes of dreams in a fleeting glance.
Silent shadows, yet hearts aflame,
In the quiet, we call your name.

Through the silence, a truth we find,
Voices unheard, yet so aligned.
Every heartbeat, a rhythmic song,
In the silence, we all belong.

In the spaces where words hold weight,
We gather strength from a silent fate.
With unspoken ties, our spirits soar,
In the quiet moments, we seek for more.

With every pause, a world unfolds,
In the silence, we are bold.
For in the hush, our hearts can share,
The beauty of life, we find it rare.

So let us listen, let us embrace,
The voices in silence, a sacred place.
In the quietude, we find our song,
Together as one, where we belong.

Soul's Embrace

In the quiet of night, we find our peace,
Whispers of dreams that never cease.
In shadows where secrets gently weave,
Two souls entwined, together we believe.

With open hearts, we share our light,
Guiding each other through the darkest night.
A bond unbroken, soft as a sigh,
In this embrace, we learn to fly.

Time may test, but we remain strong,
In each fleeting moment, we belong.
Hand in hand, we'll brave the storm,
In each other's arms, we keep warm.

The world may change, but love is true,
In every heartbeat, I find you.
Together we dance, a celestial grace,
In this universe, our souls embrace.

Bonds Beyond Time

Across the ages, our spirits blend,
In every heartbeat, a timeless friend.
Through lifetimes lived, we often meet,
In laughter and tears, our hearts repeat.

A thread unbroken, a silent pact,
In worlds unknown, in dreams intact.
The echo of love is strong and clear,
In every moment, I draw you near.

Seasons change, but we remain,
Through joy and sorrow, through loss and gain.
Each memory a star that lights the sky,
In the fabric of time, together we fly.

As the clock ticks, we carve our space,
Eternal moments, a warm embrace.
No distance can sever this bond we hold,
In every story, together we're told.

The Fabric of Kinship

Threads intertwine, a colorful weave,
In the tapestry of life, we believe.
Each strand a story, a hand to hold,
In the warmth of kinship, our hearts unfold.

Through trials faced, we stand as one,
In laughter shared, our battles won.
A circle unbroken, strong and bright,
In the darkest moments, we find the light.

With family bonds, we rise and soar,
In every heartbeat, we crave more.
Through years that pass, our love will grow,
In every encounter, let it show.

From roots deep planted, we blossom wide,
In the garden of life, love is our guide.
Through every season, come joy or strife,
In the fabric of kinship, we weave our life.

Hidden Echoes

In whispers of dusk, we seek the sound,
Footprints of memories, buried, unfound.
Through hills of longing, our voices play,
Echoes of love that never fade away.

Amidst the silence, a song unfurls,
In shadows' dance, the past twirls.
Like leaves on the wind, we softly sway,
In the hidden echoes, we find our way.

Each moment cherished, though time may flee,
In the heart of night, you're still with me.
Beneath the stars, we wander free,
In the depths of silence, just you and me.

So let the echoes resonate bright,
In the canvas of dreams, we'll paint the night.
Through hidden passages, we'll always roam,
In the depths of our hearts, we are home.